DIY Cannabis Extracts

Make Your Own Marijuana Extracts with this Simple and Easy Guide

Chris Jones

If you are looking to grow your own Marijuana, do check out our most popular book on Amazon

<u>Growing Cannabis Indoors: Grow Your Own Marijuana Indoors With This Simple And Easy Guide</u>

Get a FREE book on "How To Grow Marijuana"
http://growmarijuana.weebly.com/

Table of Contents

Introduction

First off, that you for purchasing the book *DIY Cannabis Extracts.*

This book contains proven steps and strategies on how to make your own cannabis extracts right in your very home.

You will be able to use the cannabis extracts just as you would cannabis in order to feel a different sort of "high" than you would by using cannabis the regular way. There are multiple ways that you can make cannabis extracts and smoke them.

Please make sure that you do not use faulty equipment or anything that you do not know how to use. If you are not sure how to use something, please do the research that is necessary in order to gain the proper knowledge that you'll need.

It's time for you to become an amazing expert on making your very own cannabis extracts.

Thank you and good luck!

Chapter One: What is Cannabis Extract

We all know that cannabis is a herb that flowers and produces what is known as buds that can be smoked for either medical or non-medical use. (If you live in an area in which cannabis is not legal, it is not recommended that you be in possession of anything that is cannabis related.)

Cannabis extracts are the extracted oils that you can get from a cannabis plant and use the same way that you would the cannabis, except that they will give you a different feeling than you would experience from normal cannabis.

Extracts can come in either oil form, dabs, canna butter, edibles, or many others. Each has its own specific way to be made and each has its own property that can cause varied effects on your body.

Please note that if you have not used cannabis before it is not recommended that you do so lightly. Make sure that you do all your research so that you are not potentially harming yourself because of the processes that are used to make the different extracts and possible medical conditions that you have.

Be careful with each extraction process as some are going to be more dangerous than others. And, as noted above, if you live in an area in which cannabis is illegal, please do not use any of these processes or be in possession of cannabis for your own safety as well as those around you.

Even if you do live in an area that where it is legal to possess anything that is cannabis related, please make sure that you know the specific rules and laws as to what you're allowed to do and not allowed to do. You may be allowed to have cannabis, but you may not be able to have some equipment that is required to make some of the extracts.

Also, it is important for you to try and make your own extracts or have someone that you highly trust. This is for your own safety as well as to make sure that you know exactly what is going into your extracts.

Chapter Two: How to make Cannabis Oil

Cannabis oil is actually made from cannabinoids (THC and CBD) that can be extracted from a cannabis plant. The substance of cannabis oil is actually a rather thick and sticky substance.

Cannabis oil is actually made by separating resins that you obtain from the cannabis flower by using an extraction process. This is one of the most popular cannabis extracts that you can make.

Cannabis oil can actually be used to help with medical conditions that many people suffer from such as cancer, Crohn's disease, gout, diabetes, pain relief, fibromyalgia, asthma, arthritis, migraines, and many other diseases.

It is thanks to the antioxidant properties in cannabis oil that will help you to treat and maybe even prevent some inflammatory and autoimmune diseases.

Now, when you're making cannabis oil, you first must prepare your workspace. It is important that you have an open environment so that any fumes can be blown out of the work area and not harm you. You should also make sure that you have a fire extinguisher on hand due to the highly flammable situation you will be placing yourself in. Try and stay away from propane or any other highly flammable stove-top or rice cooker. It is recommended that you use electric if possible.

Your materials are going to obviously include some cannabis to extract the oil from and the solvent that you will use to get the oil. The best results will probably come from using an ounce of marijuana and a gallon of high proof alcohol. Everclear may be your best shot at this as the high proof is going to give you a very clear and potent oil once all of the solvent burns off. Do not use any alcohol such as rubbing alcohol because it will harm you!

In addition to the solvent and the marijuana you're going to need a mixing bowl, strainer, a stirring device, a spatula, an additional bowl in order to catch any liquid, syringes, and a double boiler or even a rice cooker.

Along with this, and for your own safety, you're going to need to make sure that you have the appropriate safety gear. Before you even start mixing the solvents and various other chemicals, you need to make sure that you have gloves, oven mitts and hot pads for removing things from the hot surfaces, safety glasses (in case something should blow up) and a mask to protect yourself from the harmful chemicals.

Now, once you have prepared everything, you can move on to making your oil. You're going to start by soaking the buds of cannabis that you've obtained in the solvent that you picked. Make sure that the alcohol that you've chosen is completely covering the marijuana and then some. (This should be about an inch above the cannabis sitting in the bottom of the bowl.)

At this point in time you're going to begin to mix the solvent and cannabis together. It is best that you mash the cannabis up a bit in order to try and get the solvent to completely soak the insides and outsides of the buds. This stirring will last about three minutes and is going to be what causes the THC to be removed from the marijuana.

Once you've gotten everything mixed together, you're going to strain the liquid out into the other container that you've chosen. The liquid that you're going to get out of the cannabis will be a dark green color. Try and make sure that you squeeze all the contents out of the cannabis so that you're getting all the liquid extract that you possibly can.

The first time that you strain it, you will only manage to release about seventy maybe eighty percent of the resin out of your marijuana. You're going to want to get the rest out and this is going to be achieved by straining it again.

Everything that you have in the strainer needs to go back into the bowl that you first mixed your solvent and cannabis in, then you're going to resubmerge your cannabis in solvent yet again before redoing the process of stirring and mixing.

After the three minutes is up for that, you're going to restrain it and see another flow of dark green liquid coming from the strainer joining the green liquid that you got from your first wash.

At this point you're now ready to try and burn off the solvent so that your oil is now edible. For this, you'll fill your double boiler with water and then place your pan of liquid into the top of the double boiler.

Turn your burner onto the high setting and wait for it to begin to boil. When it is boiling, the solvent that you decided to use will now begin to burn off. Do not let your liquid bubble too long or you'll begin to lose what you truly want. As it bubbles, you'll wait for about twenty-five seconds as you scrape the sides of the pan to make sure none of it sticks.

If the liquid is still runny when it stops bubbling, then turn your burner to low and allow it to re-bubble. Once it re-bubbles, turn the burner off. Your liquid should become similar to a syrup like substance now that all the alcohol has gone out of the mixture.

Allow your oil to cool and as it cools, it will begin to thicken more.

The same process is used when you're using a rice cooker.

Now, in order to easily store the oil, you can fill a plastic oral syringe. If this does not appeal to you, then you can place the oil in an air tight container (preferably glass) and then store it in a cool, dark place.

Chapter Three: How to make Dabs

Dabs is a type of high grade hash that is normally made using butane. It can also be described as an extract from a marijuana plant that is concentrated into a smokable oil. Basically, the THC is pulled from the bud by using a solvent such as butane and what is left behind is a sticky oil like substance that can be called as shatter, wax, or some other names.

When you make dabs or smoke dabs, it is usually called dabbing. The extraction process is extremely dangerous, but it is said to be well worth the product that you get by some who have done dabbing. The most dangerous part of making dabs is the fact you're using solvents such as butane and possibly setting yourself up to cause an explosion. It is best that if you're going to make dabs, you do it in an open environment!

Dabs give a high dose of medicine to people who suffer from extreme nausea or chronic pains because it gives them the most immediate effect in helping with their ailment.

In order to make dabs, you're going to need a bottle of the highest isopropyl alcohol that you can find. This will usually be ninety-one or ninety-nine percent, two different sized trays, a knife, filter paper and a rubber band, two sealable mason jars.

Simple enough right?

Well remember that this can still be highly combustible so you need to do this in a very well ventilated area and ensure that you will not be around something that could spark. If you're in the proper area, you can do this outside to allow the fresh air to help keep the fumes down.

Before you even start, make sure that you have taken your bud and placed them into the mason jar. After this you're going to pour your alcohol into the jar covering the plant but not enough to make it so that there is standing alcohol above your plant.

Once you have this done, you're going to need to seal your jar and shake it so that the plant thoroughly gets coated (about twenty seconds) and after you've shaken it, you're going to strain the liquid that you've poured into the plant matter into another jar so that your cannabis stays in the first jar. (you can reuse this up to three times to make more dabs).

Now, you're going to boil water -in a different room because it's flammable remember-. But, once you've gotten the water boiled, fill one of your pans about halfway full with the water.

Next you'll need to pour the liquid that you've filtered off your cannabis plant into the other tray before placing that tray on the one that is currently holding the water.

In order to speed up your process, you'll want to replace the boiling water once it cools.

When you have just a sticky residue left you'll use the knife to cut the oil out of the pan and place it into the container of your choosing. Wait about thirty minutes for this process to be completed in order to ensure all the alcohol is truly off the dabs before you try and smoke them.

Chapter Four: How to make Canna butter

Canna butter or Cannabis Butter is a cannabis infused butter. This canna butter can actually be used in recipes such as brownies or cookies or even any recipe that calls for you to use butter. (Since you're already using butter for the canna butter, why not kick up your recipe with a little extra kick). It is also believed that the consumption of canna butter is better for your health than to inhale any smoke that you would if you were to just smoke regular cannabis.

When you go to make cannabis oil, it is important to know that you're basically just going to be extracting the "butter" from the marijuana by getting it into oil form before you solidify it. The biggest reason you're able to re-solidify it is because the THC is going to stick to the fat in the butter that you're going to use.

To make canna butter or weed butter, you're going to need to acquire some Tupperware and their matching lids, a saucepan, a cheesecloth or strainer, a spoon, some butter (somewhere around a pound of butter for every ounce of weed), and then of course, your weed.

Now, in order to start this process, you're going to boil some water while making sure that the cannabis that you've chosen stays floating at all times. It should stay about an inch to an inch and a half from the bottom of the pan so that it doesn't burn.

After it's begun to boil, you'll add your butter into the pan. Make sure that your butter doesn't burn either! If you begin to see signs of burning, turn your heat down to medium so that the water continues to boil and melt the butter, but not burn it.

At the point in time that your butter is melted, you're going to add your cannabis to the mixture. Make sure that you have your stove set on low for this portion of the recipe. While it's "cooking" you're going to occasionally stir the mixture until you begin to see bubbles.

Continue to allow your mixture to simmer while placing your cheesecloth over a Tupperware container and securing it with a rubber band. It is best that you use two pieces of cheese cloth so that you can ensure that you catch everything you do not want in your butter.

Wait until your water turns glossy and has a thick looking consistency. After it does, pour your mixture through the cheesecloth to separate the butter from the cannabis pieces. (use multiple bowls if necessary). Once your pan is emptied, you'll remove the cheesecloth, straining it for any remaining fluids.

Beware of small pieces of bud getting into the liquid.

Now, in order to complete your process, you'll place a lid on your container and place it in the fridge most likely just overnight. This is going to separate the canna butter and the water that you used in the beginning.

When the next day has come, you're going to get rid of all the water from your canna butter. Remove the Tupperware from the fridge and place a strainer in the sink just in case some of your butter decides to fall out. This will ensure you're not going to waste any.

You may have to squeeze the sides of the dish in order to get all the water from the bowl so that you can get a clean cut of canna butter.

After all the water is out, you can now get set to making those special brownies that you've been craving.

Make sure that any butter you don't use gets returned to the fridge to keep it good.

You should also make sure you take care of yourself after you have ingested something edible that has been made from THC. The high from it is more intense than the regular smoke and you're going to want to limit yourself as to how much you actually eat.

It is recommended that you do not drive after consuming edibles and that you just stay home and ride out your high that could last up to eight hours depending on your tolerance level as well as the THC content of the cannabis that you used.

Chapter Five: How to make Edibles

Just like the name suggests, edibles are going to be weed extracts that you can ingest. Just like we discussed in the previous chapter with weed butter. When you look at the category of edibles would be things such as pot brownies, hash brownies, canna butter, and bhang.

When you make edibles, you're using the THC in order to have a psychoactive experience, it doesn't matter if the marijuana is medical or recreational. Just like the processes that we've talked, you're going to have to heat the cannabis to a relatively high heat in order to cause decarbonxylation and extract the THCA (tetrahydrocannabinolic) acids.

In places like India, recipes can require cannabis that is sautéed in the traditional ghee before it is placed in the recipe with other ingredients. It can be boiled into tea or even placed into milk.

When you boil it in tea, you are dulling the effects of the psychoactive cannabinoids because of the water. However, when you mix it with milk, the properties of the milk are going to make it more efficient in activating the psychoactive properties.

Most of the time, when people think of edibles, it is going to be pot brownies. There are two ways that you can make the brownies; either by using oil or butter. In order to give you the proper information, I will give you both recipes so that you can see the difference and make your own choice on which one you prefer.

Oil method

You'll need a spoon, brownie mix, frying pan, a filer of some sort whether it be a strainer or a coffee filter, a grinder, some oil that isn't olive oil, and of course like always, your weed. For this recipe you're probably going to need somewhere around 2.5 grams per serving.

When using the whole box, you're going to need to grind up the weed with your grinder until it is something that resembles a powder.

After you've done this, you're going to need to place the powder in the frying pan making sure to cover the entire bottom of the pan so that you're not burning some and other bits aren't getting cooked properly. It is important that your pan matches your burner size because this is where you're going to be extracting the THC.

Add in your oil by pouring it directly onto your powder but make sure that you use the amount of oil that the brownie mix calls for. Your burner should be turned on to the lowest setting that you can get it on.

This is going to be left to sit for about six hours but can be pulled off at about two hours. But, even though you're leaving it to sit. You're going to need to make sure that you stir the mixture together about every thirty minutes so that you're not burning your oil or weed.

After you've pulled your mixture off the burner, you're going to filter the oil out so that you no longer have the weed powder mixed into the oil. The oil should be something of a brown color.

Now that you've done all this, you're going to make your brownies just as the box instructs. When you mix in the oil, you're going to use your THC infused oil so that you're getting the feeling that you want.

Butter method

The ingredients for this recipe are going to be the same as the oil method except you're going to need some butter. You can find the recipe for making the canna butter in a previous chapter, you'll also need to use pots instead of a frying pan.

Of course, before you're able to make the brownies, you'll need to extract your THC. So, you'll need to place your smaller pot inside your larger pot and throw in your butter so that you can melt it down.

Try and make sure that you don't burn your butter or else you'll end up making regular brownies because you'll have removed all the THC.

After everything is thoroughly melted, you'll remove any pieces of marijuana that is left since it no longer contains THC. You'll then proceed to spread the butter throughout the bottom of the pan that you're going to place your brownie mix in.

Cook for thirty minutes to half an hour at three hundred and fifty degrees.

Allow both recipes of brownies to cool before consuming.

Hash brownies

These are very similar to regular brownies that we just gave you the recipe for. But, the effects will not hit you for possibly forty-five minutes which will make you want to eat more. However, you're not going to need to or else you could end up finding that things could get rather messy.

In order to make hash brownies, you're going to need about four ounces of canna butter, half a teaspoon of baking powder, two ounces of self-rising flour, the rind of an orange that has been grated, eight ounces of brown sugar, two eggs, an ounce and a half of coco powder, and an ounce of ground almonds.

Along with all the ingredients, you're going to need to have some of your typical baking supplies such as a mixing bowl and spoons, however, some stuff you may find that you need before you can get to making your brownies are things like scales, wax paper, and a sieve.

For your hash brownie base, you're going to need to sieve your powders into your mixing bowl before you add in your almonds, sugar, and your orange rind.

Once you've done this, you're going to mix everything together until it is thoroughly mixed.

After that, you'll add in your butter, and eggs and then mix again until your mixture is completely smooth like a brownie mix should be.

At this point in time, you'll then place the mix into a greased lined dish and bake at one hundred and fifty degrees for about fifty-five minutes.

If you're wanting to add in some frosting for your brownies, you'll need to have four ounces of normal butter, two teaspoons of water, two ounces of coco powder, and ten ounces of confectioners' sugar.

For this, you're simply going to add all the ingredients together in a bowl and mix until they are creamy. After your brownies are done, you'll spread this over the top of the brownies.

You should be able to cut your brownies into about sixteen pieces so that they will last longer or you can share them. Make sure that you do not have more than two in the span of an hour because you're going to end up having some pretty heavy side effects, even if this isn't the first time that you've cooked with cannabis.

Cannabis Cookies

You may be realizing that you're pretty much able to add cannabis to any recipe. The important thing is that you're careful how much you add and adjust the cooking times so that you're not releasing all the THC that you're extracting in order to add it to the recipes.

Cannabis cookies are going to be similar to making chocolate chip cookies, but with a few added ingredients that you wouldn't find in normal cookies. Don't worry though, you'll enjoy them!

Make sure you gather all your ingredients that you need such as six ounces of chocolate chips, four ounces of your canna butter, two ounces of Rice Crispies, eight ounces of caster sugar, a fourth of a teaspoon of salt, one egg, half a teaspoon of bicarbonate soda, five ounces of flour and a teaspoon of vanilla essence.

Just like when making the brownies, you'll need to include equipment such as a scale and a sieve but you'll also need to have a flat cookie sheet so that you can bake your cookies properly.

If you've made cookies before, you know that this recipe is basically the same. You'll cream your butter and sugar together until you have fluffy consistency before you add in your egg, vanilla, bicarbonate of soda, and salt.

After you've mixed all this together thoroughly, you'll add in your cereal and chocolate chips until it is all mixed in properly.

Before you're able to bake them, you're going to drop a spoonful of dough onto a baking sheet until all the dough is out of your mixing bowl. Now, bake for about twelve minutes at a hundred and eighty degrees.

Bhang

In order to make bhang it is important to know that you're only using the leaves and buds from a female plant. This is a popular recipe in India and is made as a beverage rather than food or smoked.

Bhang usually is prepared in order to celebrate Holi that occurs in March as well as Vaisakhi that is celebrated in April.

When making bhang, you'll need to have seven rose petals or some rose water, one cup or rice milk or regular milk if you cannot get rice milk, a third of a cup of maple syrup, two cans of coconut milk, four tablespoons of cinnamon, one cup of cannabis buds that you've ground up, one teaspoon of poppy seeds, one tablespoon of star anise, five tablespoons of almonds, one tablespoon of cloves, and finally, two tablespoons of cardamom.

First , you're going to need to mix both your coconut milk and regular milk into a pan and stir it over a medium heat. As you continue to stir, you'll then add in your cannabis. Do not let this burn! Stir about every ten minutes or less to ensure that none sticks to the bottom of the pan.

Next you'll add in all the other ingredients making sure to stir thoroughly. Again, without letting it burn, you need to allow the mixture to simmer for about thirty minutes.

After you've allowed it to simmer, strain it off through a cheese cloth so that you can get all the cannabis and other herbs out of the tea.

Add just a sprinkle of cinnamon and serve. You can also place a cannabis leaf on top if you so desire to.

Bhang will stay in the fridge for about a week before going bad. When you're wanting to reheat it, you just add it to a saucepan and add some more milk in order to thin it out before consuming again.

Space Cakes

Space cakes are cakes or any type of pastry that contains THC. Space cakes use canna butter in order to cook so that you're getting extracted THC into your mixture.

For your space cake you're going to need anything you may want to add into your space cake such as chocolate chips, peanut butter, etc. eight grams of cannabis or hash, two eggs, half a cup of milk, a cup of non salted butter, one and three fourths cup of flour, and a cup of sugar.

The equipment you'll need is going to be a cake pan, a toothpick, a bowl, a microwave, a small plate, an oven, and a non stick spray oil.

Before you start, you'll need to preheat your oven to four hundred degrees.

While that goes on, you need to microwave your butter until it can be spread. This is usually about twenty seconds.

Next break up your cannabis by either using your hands or some kind of grinder. You'll now add it to your butter and mix it up so that your THC is saturated by the butter and can easily be extracted.

Now place all the other ingredients into your bowl and mix it with the canna butter until your batter has little to no clumps. Should you find that your batter is soggy, you're going to need to add some flower. But, if it is dry, you should add some milk.

Spray your pan with the non stick spray and pour your contents into the pan so that it is even and bakes thoroughly.

After your oven is heated up properly, you'll add in your batter so that it can be cooked. It is best that you place it on the center shelf so that all the batter gets cooked evenly.

For about twenty five minutes you'll need to find something to do, even if it is something to smoke.

After twenty five minutes, check your space cakes by placing a tooth pick into the middle of it. If it comes back clean then you have thoroughly cooked space cakes. If you have something on your toothpick, you'll need to place it back in the oven for a few more minutes. Make sure you check it periodically so that you do not burn them.

After you've taken your cake out, allow it to cool before removing it from the pan and adding your toppings,

Now you can enjoy your space cake!

Make sure you do not eat too much at one time. Space out how much you eat with in an hour so that you're not getting the effects of the extracted THC too fast or hard.

If this is your first time eating space cakes, it is best that you do not consume more than two cakes in an hour.

Chapter Six: How to make Kief

Kief is the trichomes that you will find on a cannabis plant. It can usually be shifted from the looser and drier cannabis by using a sieve. Kief is said to contain a higher concentration of THC than the flower from which you are going to remove it.

Kief can be used when making cakes or even placed in a hash like cannabis mixture. Not only that, but kief can actually be vaporized as well.

You'll need a kief press in order to extract the kief from the plant. One simple way to do this is to get two unsharpened pencils, tape, paper, and scissors.

Place a piece of tape over the head of the pencil so that you're not giving yourself lead poisoning as you use your press to gain access to the kief. Cut the tape down as close to size as you can after you've placed a strip on it to cover the lead.

Next you'll place a strip of tape to the strip of paper that you got when you were first gathering your supplies.

With the sticky side of the tape on your paper facing up, place it on a flat surface and roll the paper around one of the pencils as tightly as you possibly can get it.

Thanks to the tape being facing up, you'll keep rolling until it is completely wrapped round the pencil therefore leaving you with a cylinder shaped piece of paper.

Now that you've done this, you'll need to pull the cylinder towards the end of the pencil so that part of it is hanging off the pencil.

Using your newly formed scoop, you'll need to get some of the kief that you've collected from the bud. It is up to you with how much you place in your press.

You'll need to get all the extra kief out of the end of the pencil so that you can have an even surface to work with.

At this point in time, you'll use the end of the other pencil and place it into the cylinder. You'll need to apply some pressure for about ten seconds.

Your finished product should be a small puck like piece of kief. Now, you have the option to place your kief into a vaporizer or to smoke it in a bowl. If you're going to run it in a vapor, you'll end up having it last longer. It is important to know that you're going to need to run it at a lower temperature.

The great thing about kief is that you're not going to need any solvents so it is a safe process you can do indoors.

Chapter Seven: How to make Bubble Hash

This process is called bubble hash because ice and water are used to separate the THC from the plant. The extract that you get is going to be soft and extremely potent. It will also melt when any flame is placed near it.

After harvesting, you'll need to separate the sugar leaves from your buds. Any leaves that are yellowed or fanned out need to be removed because you're not going to want anything that has resin on it.

Please remember that you need to use some high quality sugar leaves that are wet in order to make this process work properly. If you were to use dry leaves, the process would not be the same and you would end up having more plant fall through into your hash.

After you've trimmed your sugar leaves, place them in a freezer. It is best if you keep your strains separated so that you can either make a pure hash or a special mixed creation.

Since your leaves are now frozen, you'll be ready to make some bubble hash. Before you can do anything, you need to line your bucket with either a one or five gallon bag.

Then you'll need to add your crushed ice in the bottom of your bucket and then top with your frozen sugar leaves. Crushed ice is going to work best for this process.

After you've placed your leaves in the bucket, add another lay of ice and then another layer of sugar leaves before adding the final layer of ice.

Now is when you'll add cold water to the edge of the bucket and allow it to sit.

When it is ready, you'll use a strainer like any other extract process and remove the leaves from the water. You should have a bubbly like substance that you can then melt when you get ready to smoke it.

Chapter Eight: How to make Tincture

Tincture is a process in which you use alcohol to extract the THC from the cannabis plant. In order for it to be effective, you're going to have to use an alcohol solvent that is at the very least twenty-five percent alcohol. The highest that the alcohol can be is sixty percent.

Solvents for making tincture can be things that are not necessarily ethanol. You can also use things such as propylene glycol, diethyl ether, glycerol, and even vinegar. However, not all of these solvents can or should be consumed by a human being.

In order to make tincture, you're going to need to purchase the proper proof of alcohol. Vodka is usually used in order to make tincture due to it being odorless, flavorless, and even colorless. But, if you're not wanting to use vodka, you can also substitute it with whiskey, brandy, or even rum.

As mentioned above, your alcohol content needs to be between twenty-five to sixty percent. So, when purchasing alcohol, you'll want it to be around eighty proof.

If you absolutely refuse to use alcohol due to medical or personal reasons, you can also use a high quality of apple cider vinegar or glycerin.

After you've obtained the proper solvent, you'll need to have a glass jar that can be closed. If you even wanted to, you could get darkly colored glass bottles that you can place a lid or some type of closing piece on in order to prevent air from entering your concoction.

If you want to, you can measure how much cannabis that you're wanting to place in your mixture, however, you can also just eyeball the measurements. Whichever method you decide to use; you're going to need to cover it with alcohol so that it is completely submerged.

You're going to need to stir the herbal mixture with a butter knife ensuring that you remove any and all air bubbles from it.

Once you're sure that you have gotten all the air bubbles out, then you'll need to seal your container and place it into a cool dark area such as a cupboard.

The storing process for tincture is going to be around eight eights to even a month. It is important that you shake the container about twice a day so that you're getting it mixed up properly.

You may also want to write the date that you made on the bottle so that you know when it was made so that you can also tell when it is properly steeped.

Note: please keep out of the reach of children and pets!

After the steeping process is done, you'll need to strain out the alcohol from your cannabis. Just like with any method, you're not going to want any cannabis in your alcohol because it is essentially useless now that the THC has been pulled from it.

Use something such as a spoon to make sure that you're getting all the liquid from your marijuana and not wasting any.

At this point in time you're going to replace it in jars -such as the dark colored ones I mentioned earlier- and label it with the date that you've made it.

If you do not plan on using the tincture for a while, you may want to seal the bottle with wax to make sure that no air is able to get in and ruin the mixture.

Now feel free to store your tincture until you're ready to use it. The shelf life for tincture is about five years due to the alcohol that you used in making the mixture.

Chapter Nine: How to make Rosin

Rosin is the resin that you can obtain from things like trees and even cannabis. It is usually used in vaporizers and is either black or yellow in color. Rosin can be rather brittle when stored at room temperatures and will automatically melt when put near a flame.

The reason that rosin is popular is because it is a rather affordable way to get resin and the fact that there are only a few tools that you need in order to make it most of which you may be able to find around your very home.

You're going to be using heat and pressure in order to extract the resin from the marijuana like many of the other processes that we've discussed.

First you're going to need to gather up some parchment paper, a screen (twenty-five u micron screen works best), a flat iron, your cannabis (either the flower or even bubble hash will work), and a device such as a razor blade.

You'll need to cut your parchment paper down into four by eight strips while preheating your flat iron to about two hundred degrees. It is important to remember that the lower your temperature is, the better your end result will be.

For example, if you heat your flat iron up between two hundred and fifty degrees and three hundred degrees you'll end up with more flavor and less yield. But, your rosin is going to be more stable.

However, on the other hand, if you use heat between three hundred and three hundred and thirty five degrees, your rosin is going to be filled with less flavor but will have more yield and the end result will be less stable.

Now you're going to take some of the cannabis that you broke down into .2-.5 increments and wrap it around the micron screen. Then you'll place your screen on your parchment paper before folding it so that the product is in the center of the parchment paper.

At this point in time, you're going to place the parchment paper on the flat iron and apply pressure for about five seconds.

After your time is up, you'll remove the parchment paper and unfold it. Everything that is around your product that you initially started with will be rosin. You can now remove the cannabis, but make sure to leave your rosin behind.

You'll need to take your collection device and remove the rosin so that you've got it to allow it to settle and you can smoke it however you want when it is complete. The best way to smoke rosin is in a vaporizer.

Try and keep your rosin away from heat unless you are wanting to melt it down to smoke it. If you place it in any warm environment, you'll find that your rosin will be melted when you come back to smoke it.

Chapter Ten: How to make Rick Simpson Oil (RSO)

Rick Simpson is a man who was able to take the ingredients of cannabis oils and cure himself of metastatic cancer in 2003. Ever since then, he has been trying to help prove that hemp oil is not as harmful as people like to say it is.

Not only does he have the Canadian authorities fighting him, he also has government agencies, pharmaceutical companies, and even UN Offices. But, that has not stopped him. Despite all his setbacks, he has successfully and free of charge treated about five thousand patients from different forms of diseases and even conditions that many people suffer from.

It is said that his oil has been used to help with cancer, arthritis, AIDS/HIV, diabetes, multiple sclerosis, Crohn's disease, leukemia, osteoporosis, depression, insomnia, psoriasis, asthma, glaucoma, migraines, burns, to help regulate body weight, chronic pain, or even mutated cells.

The initial treatment for using cannabis oil is meant to be used for about ninety days. First you'll start out with three doses daily for your first week. The serving size is going to be somewhere around the size of a piece of rice.

The next two to five weeks you'll then double your intake to about four times a day.

Then for the remaining weeks you'll be consuming a gram of oil a day until all sixty grams are consumed.

The taste of RSO has been described as bitter with a bit of a chlorophyll taste. Probably the best way to get the oil into your body without having to deal with the taste is to place it on your lower gums and let it dissolve on its own.

Just like anything, you'll grow accustomed to the taste of the oil as you continue to take your dosage properly every day.

Now to go over how to make RSO!

You're going to want to start with about an ounce of weed that has been dried.

First, you'll need to place your dry material into a plastic bucket.

Next you're going to place the solvent that you're using over it. The solvent that you're wanting to use is completely based on what you want to use. Just remember some solvents are going to be butane, isopropyl alcohol, ether, naphtha, or water if you absolutely want to. You're going to want about two gallons of solvent in order to properly extract the THC from one pound of marijuana. But, if you're only using an ounce, you'll be fine using five hundred milliliters.

Once you've gotten the solvent in the bucket, you're going to crush the marijuana by using a clean but untreated wooden spoon or something similar. Thanks to it still being slightly dry, you're going to still be able to crush the cannabis up.

While you're still crushing the material, you're gonna add some more solvent until you have completely soaked your material. You'll stir it for about three minutes and as you do this, your notice that the THC is going to come out of the cannabis and into the liquid.

Next you'll need to strain the cannabis out of the liquid while placing the solvent into a new bucket. Just remember that you've only gotten about eighty percent of the THC out of your plant.

Once again you're going to repeat the process in order to get the remaining THC out of the plant.

At this point in time you're going to discard your plant as it is now useless. You'll strain the liquid once more by using a coffee filter.

Now is the time that you'll fill a rice cooker about three fourths of the way full before you turn it onto high heat.

Note: make sure you're in a well ventilated area! Avoid anything that could cause a spark such as a stove or a cigarette.

While the level begins to decrease inside your rice cooker, you'll need to add some water. You're doing this in order to release the solvent that is stuck in the oil.

After you've burned down to about one inch of water in the rice cooker, you're going to swirl the contents of the rice cooker until the solvent is done being boiled.

Move your burner to low so that you're not using a heat that is over two hundred and ninety degrees.

Remove the pot from the burner yet again and pour it into a stainless steel container.

Now place that container inside of a dehydrator and allow a few hours for the water to evaporate from your oil. There should no longer be any surface activity on your oil so you should be able to use it right away.

It is best that you put it into a plastic syringe so that you can easily dispense of it after you've used it.

Please keep in mind that your oil will look a lot like grease when it has cooled.

Once again, please note that you need to keep away from anything that could cause a spark such as stoves, heating elements, cigarettes, or heat guns. You're most likely going to want to set up a fan so that you can evacuate any fumes away from your pot while making sure to stay in a well ventilated area during the entire process! The only time that it is safe to not be in a ventilated area is after the process has been completed.

RSO is not CBD oil even though it can be confused for CBD oil sometimes. Unlike with CBD, RSO has THC as well as other cannabinoids that will give the user of the RSO a more euphoric session of meditation which CBD oil is not going to do on its own.

Believe it or not, CBD oil is not a psychoactive element.

There has been research that has shown that THC is therapeutic for many different conditions that one may suffer from. Due to this research it may explain as to why many patients would prefer to have the whole cannabis oil rather than the cannabinoid oils.

Unfortunately, people are going to produce RSO and use Rick Simpson's name just to scam you out of money. Either make the oil yourself as we've instructed in this book or buy it directly from Rick's website. If you see anything that has to do with the Phoenix Tears Foundation when you're trying to buy RSO, it is not from Rick Simpson as he does not have any association with this foundation.

Rick Simpson's official website is **www.phoenixtears.ca** in which you can find more information about his RSO and how it works as well as how to make it, buy it, and many other valuable pieces of information as to how cannabis oil is good for you.

As stated above in this chapter, it is suggested that you do three doses of RSO a day when you first start out. It is recommended that you take it first thing in the morning when you wake up and then again sometime in the afternoon after eight hours have passed. But, when it comes to your final dose of the day, take it right before bedtime.

You most likely will not feel any effects of the oil until an hour after you've ingested the oil.

Conclusion

Thank you again for purchasing this book! We greatly appreciate it!

I hope this book was able to give you the appropriate information that you needed so that you can make your own cannabis extracts.

The next step is to find out which extract it is you're wanting to accomplish making and make it. Please make sure that you use the appropriate safety procedures as well as equipment so that no one gets harmed in the process of making any extracts.

I wish you the best of luck in this pursuit and hope that my information was helpful to you.

Finally, if you enjoyed this book, then I'd like to ask you for a favor, would you be kind enough to leave a review for this book on Amazon? It'd be greatly appreciated! Thank you and good luck!

Preview Of Our Popular Book "Growing Cannabis Indoors"

"Growing Cannabis Indoors: Grow Your Own Marijuana Indoors With This Simple And Easy Guide"

Are you someone who enjoys good cannabis and wants to try growing it at home?

Or maybe you require marijuana for medical purposes and want to grow it indoors?

Whatever be your reason, this book was written to teach you to grow marijuana indoors with a simple and easy explanation. This book will be suitable for complete beginners or people who already know a thing or two about cannabis.

In this book, you will learn:

- Interesting facts you didn't know about marijuana and growing. If you're excited to start growing your own cannabis, these little known facts will make you even more interested.

- How to know what type of seeds to select. Without quality seeds, you won't get quality plants. This book will tell you all you need to know about selecting the best seeds possible.

- A guide to selecting soil and fertilizer. There are particular qualities to search for when finding the soil you will plant your seeds in, and fertilizer is considered, by some, equally important. Find out what to look for.

- Dangers to avoid when growing marijuana. As a beginner, it's easy to be unaware of threats to your plants, whether it be mold or bugs. There are simple way to avoid these dangers and this book will fill you in on how to avoid losing your harvest.

- Pruning and harvesting your crop. What good is knowing how to grow cannabis if you don't know how to get it into a useable state? I will provide you with step by step techniques for pruning your plants, tips to use, and also instructions on how to dry the buds.

- And Much, Much More!

Chapter 1: The Basics of Growing

Growing indoors is quickly becoming a popular pastime for Americans, especially since the overall attitudes toward the plants and its benefits are changing more and more each day. The reasons why it's becoming so popular are as varied as the strains of weed available nowadays. Many people find marijuana enjoyable, and it isn't as difficult as people believe to grow, which means people are becoming wise to the opportunities this presents.

With the rise of interest and experimenting in regards to cultivating (non-narcotic) plants inside the house, it stands to reason that people would eventually catch on and start growing marijuana as well, using their knowledge of house plants as a base to start from.

Things to keep in mind when considering starting a grow operation:

Many people who enjoy the occasional joint may have a hard time finding a place to get it or deal with other difficulties about society's attitude toward this useful plant. Although attitudes have come a long way, they still have far to go, and the plant gets demonized regularly. In some places, there is the legality aspect to keep in mind, and growing weed at home is highly illegal, just as selling, smoking, or buying it is. It's important to keep these laws in mind, depending on where you live, and act accordingly. One of the greatest reasons for growing marijuana at home is the joy you will get from observing the seeds you selected grow to become the most beautiful house plant of all.

Growing plants indoors can be superior to outdoor operations for a number of reasons. The plants are allowed to grow in supervised conditions without being subject to as many risks as they would outdoors from unforeseen weather conditions, pests, or other mishaps. Once the gardener has the perfect system worked out, indoor operations are a reliable way to produce high quality buds. The main challenge or inconvenience of going this route is dealing with the strong smell that is likely to occur along with the growth operation.

Cannabis for both medicinal and recreational uses is now far beyond only the earth's tropical or warm climates, so for many people who enjoy it, indoor grow setups are the only choice they have. Indoor marijuana growing has never before seen the level of popularity it is at today. It has also never been this simple or easy to grow your own high quality cannabis.

The Internet provides growers with unlimited access to advice, information, suppliers of seeds and equipment, and all the necessary implements to get started on your own garden. Of course, the best plants always come from the best seeds, so make sure you prioritize the quality of those, first and foremost.

One of the best tips for selecting seeds is choosing a variety of types. The quality of the plants you grow and how much you will get from them depends on a variety of factors, when it comes to growing indoors:

- The variety of seeds.

- The temperature and climate of the grow room.

- Whether you're using clones or seeds.

- How long it takes the plants to flower.

In this chapter we will briefly review the necessary implements you need to get started with growing your own indoor marijuana, then get into more detail on each section in the later chapters.

Light:

Growing marijuana inside has become extremely common in the past couple of decades. When it's done right, a quality crop of buds will be provided, which beats what you can find anywhere else. To grow your own weed inside requires that you use artificial lights instead of sunlight, of course. The lights usually take a lot of power and wars to run and are known as high pressure sodium (HPS) lights. You can also use LED light, metal halide, or fluorescent lights with success.

Marijuana is an adaptable plant that can grow in many different environments, but one inescapable aspect of growing is making sure the plants get a lot of light. Any effective indoor operation must prioritize this. 250 watts is the absolute minimum you should opt for, but ideally you will get lights that are two or even three times stronger than that. The more light you have, the larger, denser, and all around better harvests you will enjoy. In addition to delivering strong levels of light, the efficient grower of indoor marijuana knows to have the plants close to the light to make sure they are getting what they need on their buds and leaves. Often growers, either recreational or medical, will have a growing area or at least one to two square meters, below one powerful, high pressure sodium light of anywhere from 400 to 400 watts.

Soil:

Quality indoor rooms for growing let the plants allow the plants plenty of space to grow freely in whatever medium is chosen, but soil is most commonly used for these operations. When marijuana is grown in soil, the plants typically benefit from 25% coco fiber or perlite being included in the soil, which will allow for more quality aeration. But there are a number of other additions you can use to increase the success rate.

Watering:

One mistake that is commonly made my beginner growers is giving plants grown in soil too much water. While growing, you will learn to recognize what weight your plants should be at and know when they could use more water. If you water soil marijuana plants too often, you will not only slow down the flowering process but also get a lower quality and yield from the cannabis plants.

Plant feeds or nutrients for marijuana:

Indoor marijuana growing operations means needing to be educated about plant feeds, which isn't as complicated as it may sound on the surface. All this will do is allow the roots of your plants to receive necessary nutrients and contribute to their overall quality and growth. Whether the roots are growing in a hydroponic system, clay pebbles, or coir, these nutrients are needed. Even plants that are grown in soil must have nutrients added when the soil has been sapped of what nutrients it already delivers naturally.

Make sure you are reading the labels to find nutritional information and don't succumb to the temptation to go above the levels of recommended nutrients for new plants. Newbies want their plants to grow big and strong so often want to add more than enough fertilizer to the plants, but this is not a smart move. More experienced growers eventually learn to observe their plants and know by how they look whether they require additional nutrients or need to be watered.

This book was written with the intention of being easily understandable, even to the layman, and tries not to delve into any gardening or botany techniques that are too advanced for a beginner. After reading this book, the average person should be able to start their own grow operation, even if they knew nothing about how it worked before reading.

To read more of this book, please search for it on Amazon:

Growing Cannabis Indoors: Grow Your Own Marijuana Indoors With This Simple And Easy Guide

FREE BOOK

Subscribe below to get the free book "How to Grow Marijuana".

http://growmarijuana.weebly.com/

37251919R00042

Made in the USA
San Bernardino, CA
13 August 2016